Fluent in Blue

Fluent in Blue

poems

Erin Murphy

GRAYSON BOOKS
West Hartford, Connecticut
graysonbooks.com

Fluent in Blue
Copyright © 2024 by Erin Murphy
Published by Grayson Books
West Hartford, Connecticut
ISBN: 979-8-9888186-6-3
Library of Congress Control Number: 2024932958

Book and Cover Design by Cindy Stewart
Cover Image © Dmitry/Adobe Stock
Author Photo by Molly De Prospo

For Rich

Acknowledgments

Thank you to the following journals that originally published these poems, sometimes with different titles or formatting:

"The Internet of Things," *Rattle*

"Azul," *North American Review*

"Sentence," *Waxwing*

"Impala," *Passages North*

"In Gear," *Paterson Literary Review*

"After/Before," *Diode*

"The World is a Scented Handkerchief," *SWWIM*

"Flood," *Memoir*

"Once You've Seen a Bird in Your House," *Narrative Northeast*

"Vaughn," *Jellyfish Review*

"Among the Beasts," *Unbroken*

"I Knew a Pyromaniac," *ONE ART: a journal of poetry*

"The Week My Son Leaves Home," *Literary Mama*

"Aperture," *The New Verse News*

"The Strip Mall of Second Chances," *New World Writing*

"Concealed," *New World Writing*

"Dear London Neighbor," *Midwest Quarterly*

"Ghazal for Irvo Otieno," *ONE ART: a journal of poetry*

"Son Mother Blues," *Summerset Review*

"18-Year-Old Daughter as Runaway Horse," *Mom Egg Review*

"Anthimeria," *North American Review*

"Dear Rita," *ONE ART, a journal of poetry*

"Aftermath," *The New Verse News*

"That First Summer," *About Place*

"I-95 Corridor," *Rattle*

"The Internet of Things" won the 2021 Rattle Poetry Prize Readers' Choice Award.

"Anthimeria" and "Azul" were James Hearst Poetry Prize finalists.

"In Gear" received the Allen Ginsburg Poetry Award Editor's Choice Award.

"Vaughn" received a Best of the Net nomination.

"To the Man Who Stole Our Pregnant Dog" was featured on a podcast produced by *Brevity* and subsequently published in *ONE ART: a journal of poetry*.

"The Week After" was published in *Howl, 2016: Poems and Essays in Response to the Election* edited by Trish MacEnulty (Prism Light Press).

"Hide-and-Seek" was published in *The Strategic Poet: Honing the Craft* edited by Diane Lockward (Terrapin Books).

Thank you to Penn State University, the Penn State Altoona Advisory Board, and the Virginia Center for Creative Arts for support to complete this book.

Contents

I

The Internet of Things

(n.): the networking capability that allows information
to be sent and received by objects and devices

The low tide riverbed silt
        of things. The cloud-swept

distant hill of things.
        The open bedroom window

in spring of things.
        The moonlit cricket

symphony of things.
        The pitter-patter

tin roof rain of things.
        The fifty-year marriage

loose skin of things.
        The clipped winter light

of things. The stippled lymph
        node of things. The grief.

Oh—the grief. The brief
        ecstatic flight of things.

II

I-95 Corridor

1.
This is where I was cited
for reckless driving
and my uncle quipped
95 is the route number,
not the speed limit.

2.
This is where I stopped
with an ex-boyfriend
on the last stretch from Miami
and a motel clerk asked
if we wanted the *all night*
or *hourly* rate.

3.
This is where my grad school
U-Haul broke down and I
waited for the wrecker
with a Swiss Army knife
flexed against my bare thigh.

4.
This is where I learned
all the lyrics to Dylan's
"Subterranean Homesick Blues,"
rewinding the cassette
till it snapped in the deck.

5.
This is where I interviewed
for an adjunct teaching gig
that would cost me more
in tolls and gas than I'd earn.

6.
This is where thieves
took my Plymouth Breeze
on a joyride then dumped it
on the shoulder, my just-cashed
paycheck still in the console.

7.
This is where my husband
missed an exit for the symphony
and grazed a concrete pillar
beneath an underpass.

8.
This is where I ordered
my daughter vanilla ice cream
with extra maraschino cherries
after she lay corpse-still
for her first echocardiogram.

9.
This is where a tanker truck
caught fire, melting the highway's
steel beams until an entire span
collapsed like a ruptured aorta.

10.
Corridor:
a long,
narrow
passage
between
rooms
or land.
Or time.

11.
They are still sifting through
the truck driver's remains.

12.
I can never remember
if it's steel oneself
or steal oneself. Am I
supposed to harden my feelings
or shove them under
my shirt like a shoplifter?

13.
In the show I'm watching,
one corridor leads
to another, rough cut
after rough cut of white walls
in a workplace maze.

14.
The day of the symphony,
we abandoned our SUV
on the off-ramp and ran
four blocks to the concert hall,
plunking into plush seats
just in time for *da da da dum*.

15.
Commute, hospital, concert,
wedding, commute, bar mitzvah,
commute, funeral, commute.

16.
Lately I need to sit
closer to the throat
of a bass trombone

or purring cat to feel
a stirring in my pulse.

17.
My uncle is gone now,
a stroke two days
before Christmas.

18.
For years I replayed
that last conversation
in my ex's red Jetta,
his hands trying to bend
the steering wheel,
his eyes swollen.

19.
What's the difference
between carefree
and careless?

20.
I'm not sure
I want to know.

21.
So many bodies
and bodies in motion.

22.
I can't steal myself.
I'm already stolen.

I Knew a Pyromaniac

A neighborhood boy,
barely old enough to sit

at the kitchen table
without a booster seat.

He couldn't tie his shoes
but lit a match with one

flick of a slim wrist.
He sniffed sulfur on his

fingers the way most kids
inhale the smell of warm

chocolate chip cookies.
His father was gone—

not dead, just gone. This
we shared. His mother

was the shadow of a shadow.
First a swing set burned.

Then a garden shed. And
then they moved. Once

when I was babysitting him,
he sat on my lap and drew

a picture of a girl. *Who's that?*
I asked. He pointed.

You. I was on fire. He didn't
know how to hold a crayon.

But he knew the hottest
part of the flame was blue.

To the Man Who Stole Our Pregnant Dog

I hope she bit you, shredding the flesh
of the hand that wooed her from my childhood

yard. You probably sold her pups off the back
of a rusty truck at a flea market, a handwritten

sign missing an *s* or a *t* in *Bassett Hound*.
What I remember: her banana peel ears

swept the ground like unhemmed drapes.
We called her Blarney, and I'd already

named the babies after other Irish castles
from the set of pleather-bound Britannicas

we bought by the month. Every evening
for weeks, I sat in the bath after the water turned

cold, thinking my discomfort would bring her
home. The walls shuddered with the last

rumblings of my parents' marriage. I slid
under to see how long I could go without air,

the soapy surface a scrim over a body
that was there, then not there.

Among the Beasts

We packed picnics—Ritz crackers and grapes,
bottles of Coke—and sat among the dead:

a beloved beagle who was now *chasing balls*
in heaven, a 20-year-old calico *gone too soon.*

Graves were marked with lacquered photographs
and poems, cracked and yellow from the sun.

Someone had buried a horse. Its tombstone
was a life-sized thoroughbred reigning over

the smaller beasts. This was pre-Stephen King,
pre-zoning that would prohibit a pet cemetery

in the center of a subdivision. Once we saw
a funeral for a German shepherd. The owner—

a teary middle-aged man—peeled back
a black garbage bag to reveal a stiff head,

an open jaw. I thought of the science experiment
from class: our teacher dipped a goldfish

in liquid nitrogen, then shattered it on his desk,
bits of orange scattering like glass. The boys

laughed. In that brief moment of shock, I darted
to collect the shards and reassemble them

like a puzzle or a memory. Then the teacher asked
for a volunteer to scoop the pieces into the trash.

Impala

for Stephanie

Kickball on my dead-end street,
you bowling the red rubber ball,
me launching it toward that recurring
suburban sky. Then creeping by:

the beige sedan, hovering and purring
like the *Close Encounters* mother ship.
Impala. And all I could think was *pale*,
pale as the ass of the man who flashed

us, then fled, slipping our stunned faces
into his pocket like a snapshot, leaving us
with a lifetime of taking license plates
whether we needed them or not.

Flood

I grew up in the capital
of the Confederacy,

my skin darkened
only by the shadows

of Monument Avenue.
Once the James River

flooded and the two whitest
boys from my high school

ignored warnings
and tooled around

in a canoe until the waters
took them. For days

their buttoned-down
faces were on the news

as helicopters swooped
and searched. They were

found clinging to a tree,
muddy and cold but unhurt.

More than a house
with a pool in the suburbs.

More than tuition
at a brick college

with a cupola. More than
a guided hunting trip

to Alaska where you sleep
in a luxury yurt. That's

how much the rescue cost.
They did not think:

moonlit bank where
my ancestors were

dragged from ships
or *branch from which*

bodies once swung.
They did not have to.

They did not have to
question their worth.

In Gear

The first time I drove a stick shift
        alone, I had my newly laminated
license shoved in the back pocket

of my cut-off jeans. I bucked up
        and down our cul-de-sac in Mom's
neon orange Pinto. Late June,

99 degrees, my thighs suctioned
        to the black vinyl seats. By noon,
ready to brave the neighborhood,

I coasted along Pamela Drive
        and made it all the way to Hart Road
when the car cleared its throat

and stalled. Within a month,
        I would be fluent in the language
of manual transmission, my hands

and feet finding their own perfect
        choreography. On my way to work
at the ice cream parlor, I'd stop

at the 7-11 for a Diet Coke. *Girl, you
        don't need to be on a diet*, the cute
cashier would wink as he rang me up.

His name was Eric. He was 24
        and going into his second year
of dental school, I would learn.

He had curly blonde hair, blue eyes,
        and a wife. Yes, a wife. But before this—
before Eric showed up at the end

of my shift and said *Meet me*
        in the parking lot, before I walked out
in that houndstooth uniform

and found him leaning against my car
        under the stars and waxing moon,
arms folded across his broad chest,

before I let him kiss me
        so hard his stubble cut my upper lip—
before this, I was stuck on that suburban

street, the Pinto's engine stuttering
        like the nervous boys I'd moved beyond.
There was more to life, I knew,

than movies and the mall and cruising
        down Broad Street past the skating rink
and all-night supermarket.

With one foot on the accelerator
        and the other clenching the clutch,
I got the goddamn thing started.

Sarah

She married the first guy who took her
away from her mercurial mother. Once

on the way to his trailer in Tappahannock,
he pulled over to the shoulder on Route 301

and said *Blow me.* He pressed her head
down until he came, then yanked

his truck into gear. That was the year
we graduated from high school. A week later,

we learned at the rehearsal that the organist
didn't know "Here Comes the Bride." Instead,

she'd play the "Prince of Denmark's March"
from Diana's wedding to Charles. Sarah was

in tears. How could a church organist not know
the most popular wedding processional,

my friend's only wish for the day? It was like
a fisherman not knowing how to use a worm

as bait. I could not convince Sarah to wait
for another plan—or even another man—

but dammit, I was determined to have
that organist replaced: a garden hose

sprayed to save the shed as the house
is swallowed by flames. On the wedding eve,

I tried a dozen names in the yellow pages.
I called friends of friends of friends and their

cousins. It was after 10 p.m. On the back
of my bedroom door hung my baby blue

taffeta maid of honor dress. I wept when
the small voice of a young woman said *Yes*.

Sibilant

From the Latin, *sibilans:* hissing or whistling,
as in *She sells sea shells, Sing a song of sixpence.*

Smiles and *silence* and *pleasure* and *sorrow.*
How the same tongue that shushes you to sleep

can slide so easily into a snake's vicious whisper
tomorrow. My father taught me shot put, brought chocolate

to my seventh-grade track meet for a burst of speed.
My father shut himself behind doors for days,

emerging only to eat. Some linguists insist
th, f, z, and *v* sounds are not truly sibilant,

merely half-siblings of *s*, like the daughter
my father conceived with his second wife, their marriage

a brief flutter, a flashpoint before his darkness
settled in like river mist. *Mist. Missed.*

Things I've assumed my younger brother and half-sister knew:
That his '68 Mustang was dark green, not black.

That once when it stalled on an overpass
in a freak Virginia blizzard, we slung groceries

over our shoulders and slid six blocks
to our father's basement apartment, his first since

the divorce. That the bathroom had tiles the color
of Pepto Bismol. That our father was a chemistry equation

and the ghost of chalk after the lesson is erased.
That he loved us. That he loved us all.

That First Summer

Most weekends we packed our blue canoe
with a tent, sleeping bags, books, a cooler,
and enough food and wine for the weekend,

then paddled out to a sand bar in the middle
of the river. For two days we swam and read
and drank and fucked, stretching out in the sun,

lean and dark. Later we learned that some nights
engineers release waters from the dam upstream
to control the floodplain. Experienced boaters

knew to check the schedule. What did we know?
Nothing about harnessing nature, everything
about being swept away.

London Neighbor

My extra room was desk-wide
with a view of you at work in your twin

row house across the street. We'd tap
our keyboards for hours, then meet

eyes in the safe distance between.
Mid-afternoon, you shuffled to your

saffron kitchen for a cup of tea,
the window fogging with kettle steam.

At the corner market, you could have
been any other man picking up a loaf

of bread or can of beans. I kept you in
a frame: conscience, counterweight, dream.

Practice

for Peter Gnanes, M.D.

You and your Sri Lankan lilt—
syllables rising and falling
like water in a tilted bowl—

brought both of my babies
into the breathing world.
I found you in the Yellow Pages

and stayed because you
scrawled your home number
on your business cards. Your

wood-paneled waiting room
held patients no one wanted:
teen girls, the uninsured,

women who turtled
inside men's flannel shirts.
I sat with them, leather briefcase

tucked under a tattered chair.
Years later, I gave you
a photograph of my children.

You pressed it to your chest
and closed your eyes
as if rehearsing a prayer.

My 15-Year-old Daughter Brings Home a Baby

Not a real baby but a computerized doll
that wails when he needs to be changed
or rocked or fed. There are sensors that track

how long it takes my daughter to respond,
how gently she supports the baby's head.
The cries are real cries recorded on a chip,

and six times a night we all wake
to a sound we haven't heard in years.
My daughter in her pink pajamas rolls out

of bed. Does he need a bottle? Is he wet?
It's just a weekend lesson, a school requirement
for a grade. Once when my daughter was

this age, my husband and I got in the car
and backed out into the street. *Wait,* I said,
where's the baby? Sure enough, we'd left her

in the living room strapped into her car seat.
Each of us thought the other had her, distracted
by refilling the diaper bag and putting bills

in the outgoing mail. We bolted inside
and found her asleep, completely unaware
of the first of many times we would fail.

Dear Son

Do you remember the birthday cake
in the back of the black cab? The frosting

was turquoise, bright as waves of silk
unspooled by street vendors we sped past

in North Wembley. We were late
to a Manchester United game,

the tickets your surprise gift. I flicked
the lighter but could not summon a spark.

Our driver mumbled something in Urdu,
then double-parked alongside a corner store.

Moments later he returned, cupping
in his hands a single lit match. Breath held

and steps measured, he made his way
across an invisible balance beam. A decade

earlier, I had done the same. I kissed
each of your ten candles with the flame.

Tooth and Claw

My daughter watches from the storm door
as a squirrel roots for nuts under the snow.

It digs and digs but the ground is solid.
For the third straight day, the high is

five below. A hawk juts down from the top
of a telephone pole. It makes a test run,

returns to its perch, then swoops again
to sever the squirrel's head. The snow

is seeped with red. My daughter shrieks.
The body is propped in the crotch of a maple tree,

a bloody lesson in nature and helplessness.
Soon the bird will return for the rest.

Vaughn

A boy, a boy with pimples and a coltish gait,
has died. A boy, the younger brother
of my daughter's friend, has died, has taken

his own life. I watched him play in the pool,
hour after hour of splat ball and Marco Polo,
summer after summer, as he grew taller

than his sister. Still, she'd spread his towel
to dry in the sun and wait for him at the end
of the day as he stabbed his wet feet

into flip flops. White mother, Black father
in a part of Pennsylvania where pickups
fly Confederate flags under a bruised

sky. All four of them—parents and kids—
have V names. Such hope in those names,
their own little club of safety and love.

Once Vanessa stayed at our house
for a birthday sleepover. The next morning
the girls were going to Galactic Ice,

an indoor rink that blasts pop music.
As she buttoned her coat, her $5 bill
floated to the floor and our dog ate it,

swallowed it whole. Everyone laughed
except Vanessa who cried hard, as if
she saw the entire day playing out—

her friends skate-dancing backwards
and eating French fries in the snack bar—
while she sat home alone. I scrambled

for my wallet and handed her a ten.
Her sobs turned to deep breaths. Then: calm.
How simple it was to ease her pain then.

The Week My Son Leaves Home

At the red light
I can see inside

the fast food place
with the atrium

playground. A mother
wipes the face

of a child who tries
to pry himself away

from her, eager to return
to the cylinder slide.

       Surely there is a physics model for this—

the tug and the pull.
I can feel his warm

gummy hands
in mine, sticky

with juice. I can
feel him slip loose.

18-Year-Old Daughter as Runaway Horse

Her father searches the streets and alleys,
imploring passersby with photos on his phone—
those dark eyes, the glossy black coat.

I stay behind, opening and closing the stall,
recreating sounds I hope will draw her home: tongue
click of the latch. The hinge—that low moan.

Don't Write About Herons

a poet once said, so this isn't about the blue heron
we witness in Rock Hall. It's about the argument

we're having when it lands on the breakwater,
you spitting *I'm sorry,* me saying *You're not sorry*—

you're angry as the bird, silhouetted against
the Chesapeake Bay, lifts its massive wings.

Burrowing in my own rage, I do not share
the memory it shakes loose of the time

our now-grown son's preschool teacher
insisted the pterodactyl and Pteranodon

were the same thing, leaving our child—
who'd spent half his brief life studying

herbivores and carnivores and the number of plates
on a stegosaurus—in disbelief. Did she even know

that dinosaurs couldn't sweat, that sauropods were
bigger than the T-Rex? Did she not drift off to sleep

each night debating in her mind which creature
would be left standing in a fight to the death?

Poem for My Children's Friends

This poem is for Caleb whose mother died
from an overdose the morning he was supposed

to take the SATs, who joined the Air Force
and spent three years in South Korea

and another two in Idaho where he learned
from YouTube videos how to make

dining room tables that he sold weekends
at farmer's markets in Boise.

This is for Huck Finn lookalike Cody
who'd never been outside of our small town

until we took him to Baltimore to see
The Lion King at the Hippodrome. His head

was so filled with stories of urban violence
that he thought the prongs on a bike rack

were two machine guns mounted on the back
of a Honda Civic. This poem is for Vanessa

whose baby brother shot himself in the head.
Vanessa, who stepped forward

from the commencement chorus for a solo,
all the pain and pieces of her shattered

family filling the stadium's empty spaces.
This is for Emily who got engaged

to a guy a month after she met him online.
This is for Mark whose family dresses up

in suits and flowered dresses each Sunday
morning, then sits in the living room to watch

church services on TV. Connor, who works
for Amazon and lives in a Manhattan apartment

with a rooftop pool does not need this poem.
Not yet. But I

will leave an opening for him the way I stocked
the basement mini-fridge with Gatorade

and snacks for kids who crowded the futon
to play video games, explosions and groans

and cheers wafting upstairs. Once my son
butt-dialed me from a friend's house

when a group of boys were talking
about religion. *What if,* my son asked,

*all of the stories in the Bible
are like Greek myths—you know, made up*

to explain stuff we don't understand?
I listened hard for his friends' responses

but could hear only their muffled objections.
This poem is for the friend born Laura

who transitioned during sophomore year,
who spent weeks searching

lists of boy names, trying them on like
polo shirts and khaki pants. And this is for

the AP history teacher who crossed out
Laura in her gradebook and wrote *Lance.*

When One Has Lived a Long Time in a Small Town

You see the good oral surgeon
      walking down 11th Avenue,
          the one who removed the tooth
              the bad oral surgeon screwed up.

              You still have the x-ray: the drill bit
          embedded in the root of your molar,
      a perfect corkscrew for the world's
tiniest bottle of wine. In a tavern,

you order a drink from a waiter
      who—in eighth grade gym class—
          called your son a *f*g*. As he
              delivers a flute of Prosecco

              to your booth, you feel
          a pang for the boy, now man,
      who no doubt was figuring out
if this town was big enough

for his own desires.
      At the symphony you sit
          next to the owner of a charter company
              who, back in the 70s, took fifteen buses

              to see Kiss perform in Pittsburgh.
          On the way home, it snowed,
      stranding the fleet and all
800 passengers on Route 22.

Tonight's guest performer
      is the son of a woman
          you used to know. Back then,
              he was a pre-teen who loved piano,

and now, doctorate in hand, he's back
in Altoona to play "Rhapsody in Blue"
with the local orchestra, pounding
his way to a sweat so glossy

he'll toss his slippery eyeglasses
onto the concert grand. The march
at minute five sounds like freight trains
thundering through our town, the echo

of a booming railroad empire
bouncing off brick buildings.
In a museum across the tracks,
there's a 1924 photo of Babe Ruth

who crushed the ball
from Cricket Field to Lexington
and 7th Street. Today, he would have
hit a convenience store called Sheetz.

When one has lived a long time
in a small town. By *one* I mean
you, and by *you* I mean *I*.
Once in a city far from here,

I heard Galway Kinnell read from
his book *When One Has Lived*
a Long Time Alone, and the reading
was so long that I thought, ungenerously,

No wonder you live alone, man.
And now I'm guilty of writing
long poems no one will want to hear.
I guess what I'm trying to say

is that I'm growing uncertain
          with certainty. I am certainly
                    uncertain. The good oral surgeon's
                              daughter brought home a mini pig.

                    It turns out there's no such thing
          as a mini pig. It grew to 300 pounds.
          Some pig. If that's not a metaphor for life
in a small town, I don't know what is.

My late mother-in-law, who lived
          99 years, was a concert pianist.
                    When she entertained fellow residents
                              in the senior home down the block, she closed

                    each show with "Rhapsody in Blue."
          On her 100th birthday, I woke
          to the sound of a piano at 5 a.m.
and shook my husband.

He recognized her signature
          flourishes and trills and tiptoed
                    downstairs during the bursting
                              blue-note riff of the finale.

                    But there was no one at the piano,
          just the blue-dark shadows of dawn.
          Later we'd deduce that the cat had
stepped on the CD player remote

that just happened to cue
          the recording she'd made
                    at a local studio, the owner
                              of which is running the sound board

at tonight's symphony. He says
he'll text me when his jazz band
is playing next month at Spring Dam.
Sometimes when I tell the story

of our mystery pianist, I embellish
and say my husband grabbed a bat,
building suspense with words the way
Gershwin built tension with notes.

My only ghost story, I like to say.
But when one has lived a long time
in a small town, maybe everything's
a ghost story. Maybe we're all ghosts.

Sentence

An oncoming car just misses a squirrel
which darts to a patch of grass,
picks up a black nut and begins nibbling
as if nothing has happened. My daughter asks
Do you think squirrels get that feeling
like 'I almost died'?

Thirteen months ago, my daughter
was stopped at a red light at 9:41 p.m.
when a drunk driver of a two-ton pickup
plowed into her from behind. Her car
was totaled. Her body was less damaged—
soft tissue injuries, doctors called them.
The cops said she was lucky to be alive.
The driver was handcuffed and installed
in the back of a squad car, and we returned
to our routines: school, work. She went
to physical therapy a few times a week.
There was a plea agreement, but when
the man showed up drunk to the hearing,
they sent him to prison.

I've heard that squirrels don't remember
where they buried their nuts. Chances are
when they find one, it was planted
by a fellow rodent. Sometimes when
I see a squirrel dig up an acorn in my yard,
I imagine him patting himself
on his little squirrel back and saying,
What a good idea it was for me to hide
this nut right here where I'd find it!

How easy it is to anthropomorphize
animals. How difficult to humanize some
humans. The man who hit my daughter

is a welder. I pass his shop every day
on my way to work. It seems he does
mostly routine jobs—machine parts, pipes—
but out front there are a few art pieces
on display: an eagle in flight, a tree with
cursive limbs. A scrolled arch says *For rent—
perfect for weddings.* The month he was
incarcerated, there was a handwritten note
on the door. I never got close enough to read it.

When my daughter asked about the squirrels,
I didn't think about her accident. Most days
I give the man only the smallest thought,
like my late grandmother crossing herself
as she passed a church. Other days I drive by
and it hits me—literally hits me, like I've been
slammed in the gut by an invisible battering ram.
All the air is sucked from my lungs and it's—
I—can't—I—try—she—almost—I—

III

Wrong House

A neighbor's cousin stumbles drunk
into my aunt and uncle's suburban home

at 2 a.m. Uncle Dickey trudges downstairs
in boxer shorts to discover the man dead

to the world on the good floral sofa.
Wrong house, buddy, he informs

the rum-soaked intruder, nudging him
awake. He steers the wobbly-legged stranger to

to the next split-level, knocks, and says,
I think I found something that belongs to you.

Who left the door unlocked is a matter
to be disputed at family backyard BBQs

for years to come. Aunt Patti will blame
Dickey. He'll claim she was the last one in

after feeding a stray cat. Always armed
with a funny yarn, he'll set the scene: the body

slumped on the couch, the dog looking up like
Who the hell is that? Uncle Dickey's face,

burned from tarring roofs in the sun, reddens
more with each telling. In some versions,

he mistakes the lump for his wife. In others,
he wields a phantom baseball bat. We cry

from laughing, none of us asking what would
have happened had the man been Black.

Son Mother Blues

They may as well be girls when they're young
Smooth skin, loose curls, moon eyes when they're young
Want to sleep wedged up beside you when they're young
Braid your hair, paint your nails, confide when they're young
Bellies full of questions, hungry minds when they're young
Till they learn to hide, bide their time, bite their tongues

Send a boy into the world and hope he makes it home
Send a dark boy into the dark world and hope he makes it home
Angry men waiting at every turn
Angry men with guns waiting at every turn
Angry men with guns and badges waiting at every turn
They beat you
Beat you down
Beat you down till you turn

They make you say yes
Make you say yes
Yes, sir
Yes, sir
Yes, sir
Make you say yes
Till you burn
Till we burn

Ghazal for Irvo Otieno

*Seven sheriff's deputies and three hospital workers were charged with
second-degree murder in the death of Irvo Otieno, who died during intake
at a Virginia state mental health facility.*

You and I walked the same halls of a school
named for Douglas Southall Freeman,

famed editor and Pulitzer winner
who chanted "integration never" as a mantra.

Our mascot back then was the Rebel,
a cartoonish blue & gray Confederate man.

And to this day in social media threads,
his replacement—"Maverick"—is mentioned

with scorn by those who miss rooms
filled with likeminded white men.

You were an honor student, musician,
and varsity football defensive lineman.

But naked, shackled, and cuffed, you were
no match for so many armed men.

A scrum of uniforms tackled you
like a rabid animal, not a man.

Irvo Otieno, Irvo Otieno, Irvo Otieno.
Brother, son, fellow alum, fellow human.

Soon your name, like the others, will grow
dim. Which city, which murdered Black man?

Which one had a bag of candy, a cigarette, a toy
gun in his hand? Which one tried to manifest

a long-gone mother? Which one couldn't
breathe? Which one was not yet even a man?

Dear Rita

In July 1971, Rita Curran, 24, was found strangled in her apartment in Burlington, Vt. More than fifty years later, authorities used DNA from a cigarette butt to identify her killer: her upstairs neighbor.

You were born the same year as my mother
and like my mother became a *schoolteacher,*

the language from today's news frozen in the 70s
like you. One of three careers open to girls—

yes, *girls*—back then: teacher, secretary, nurse.
Or, for the lucky ones, *stewardess* with its fantasy of soaring

far from the New England factory town where summers
were spent screwing caps onto toothpaste tubes

for a fraction of minimum wage. Your killer
was cooling off after a fight with his wife

and likely took his rage out on you. Maybe your red hair
reminded him of her. Or maybe any woman would do,

any body he could break. And then what, a smoke
in your room before trudging upstairs to crawl

in bed beside his alibi? He died decades ago, taking
these answers to his grave. In the photo, you wear

a black choker. Choker: *a necklace or ornamental band
of fabric that fits closely around the neck.* Choker:

one who chokes. If you had lived, you'd be retired
like my mother who texts me pictures of hummingbirds

at her feeder. Always the teacher, she explains
that the male's ruby throat—*gorget*—is named

for a knight's breastplate. The pale wings of females
blur against the gray sky as if they've been erased.

Hide-and-Seek

Northern Virginia, 2002

The week I teach poetry to fourth graders,
my students scramble up slides at recess

and blister their fingers on monkey bars.
They swipe the shoulders of each other's

striped t-shirts and erupt in a chorus
of *Not it! Not it!* They are not squirming

in desks, locked down because a sniper
is targeting strangers. A teen in search

of a father is not crouching in the trunk
of a blue Chevy Caprice, taking aim

at bus passengers and landscapers
and drivers pumping gas. On this day,

a 25-year-old woman vacuums Cheerios
from the back seat of her mini-van

at a Shell station and returns home
to her toddler daughter whose favorite

word is *why. Why dogs bark? Why
thunder go boom? Why babies cry? Why?*

Why? A liquor store clerk rings up
the last sale of the night and heads back

to his garden apartment where he falls
asleep to *Law & Order* re-runs.

Their families will not have to ask *why*. I write
personification on the board. *What word*

is hiding inside? I ask. I'm looking, of course,
for *person*. In this version, there is only one boy

in the world hungry for attention, and he shoots
his arm in the air and answers *cat*.

Aftermath

*After natural and man-made disasters such as earthquakes, hurricanes,
and explosions, victims may survive in voids that are formed naturally
in collapsed structures. —Science Direct*

First, look for voids:
        bathtubs, stairwells, ribcages

of infant cribs, the clumsy
        geometry of cantilevers and lean-tos

from collapsed roofs, gaps
        beneath desks where small bodies

just yesterday learned
        to add and subtract.

Next, make your own voids:
        slide flat bags between rubble

to inflate makeshift rooms
        of dusty birthday balloons.

Finally, chisel dates in your
        mind: one week, one month,

one year since you packed
        a lunch satchel and walked

your only child to school.
        This is when the void finds you.

Yearlings

Our motion detecting camera captures
        a yearling deer at 2:06 a.m. In the grainy
black and white clip, he takes tentative steps

on our square of lawn: a circus performer
        on stilts, wobbly piñata. Ears like two blades
of a ceiling fan, rear legs splayed,

knobby as the spindles of an upright Steinway.
        I read once that Victorians draped piano legs
because they looked too human,

too titillating. [*Look it up,* I would tell
        a student writing this poem.] What was I
dreaming about at that moment? Most likely

the upcoming election, how the president
        turned all our televisions black. We reached
into our empty screens to retrieve armfuls

of darkness. In class this week we read a poem
        in which the speaker compared school busses
to goldfish in a stream. *What came first,*

a young woman asked, *the busses or the fish?*
        This semester my students are a Brady Bunch
grid of faces, our class *remote* due to the pandemic.

They are taking their first steps into poetry.
        You've gotta crawl before you can walk,
people say. But my own children

never crawled. They sat like small Buddhas
        till they were almost fourteen months old,
then went straight to toddling.

It's late October. Every day I see bodies
         of deer smeared across roadways—
bloody and disemboweled, entrails rutted

by tire tracks. Sometimes one seems
         to be sleeping on the shoulder, no visible sign
of injury—clipped, no doubt, internal bleeding.

[Here's where I'd say read William Stafford:
         I thought hard for us all—my only swerving—,
then pushed her over the edge into the river.]

545 migrant children may never
         see their parents again. *Unreachable,*
our government deems them.

The yearling sniffs the sideview mirror
         of my car, then startles, as if
his name has just been called.

He leaves a brushstroke in his wake
         like breath against cold night air.
I think hard for us all.

At the End of the Day

—the phrase drained of meaning, dredged
like the local lake where carp and bass and bluegills
flap in sediment below the dam.

    [Some of the fish old enough to vote.]

At the end of the day, Mars is the brightest it's been
in a decade. After sunset, look east for the rusty tinge.

    [Its surface rich in iron oxide.]

At the end of the day, a call from the grown daughter
still on your cell phone plan, her cheek pressed against glass
fitted by a worker who solders three screens a minute,
twelve hours a shift.

    [*Solders*, so close to *soldiers*.]

At the end of the day, a once-feral cat falls asleep
in your lap, its prehensile paw gripping your hand.

    [Is *hensile* a word?]

At the end of the day, the wheatfield is still
flattened by the minivan that careened
off the road in a head-on crash.

    [Tinny sirens in the distance, blood
    on the steering wheel, blood in the mouth.]

At the end of the day, children are sleeping
on concrete, covered only by Mylar blankets
the color of shiny dimes.

    [Think March of Dimes, dime bag.]

At the end of the day, darkness is a room
we double-lock with a rusty key.

[I've used rusty twice. I really don't care, do you?]

At the end of the day we can't let ourselves dwell
on the fish or the children.

[*Sediment*, so close to *sentiment*.]

At the end of the day, I dream our kitchen counters
are too high. We raise the floors, plank by grainy
wooden plank, like lake water after a storm.

[At the end of the day, we have a granite island,
a Cuisinart toaster oven, an electric tea kettle.]

The fish can't be relocated, something about invasive species.
The parents can't be located, something about
cruel bureaucracies.

[At the end of the day, he knew,
they knew, we knew.]

At the end of the day, blood tastes like metal.

[Does metal taste like blood?]

At the end of the day, I retreat to the luxury
of pin-fitted syllables on a page.

[*Page*, so close to *cage*.]

At the end of the day, we all seek our own level.

Aperture

November 2020

The cloud bank is a mountain—
no, a continent—in the gun metal

sky and beneath it a cavalry
of trees, mostly oak, limbs rhyming

in *Vs*. Look closer to see the anarchy
of leaves—some refusing

to surrender even after three nights
of frost. What will it take?

Remember the film in which
the boys were cloned from evil DNA.

Remember half your neighbors
voted for—and from—hate.

Who has won? Who has lost?
Zoom in to the tip of a twig

where a caterpillar—backlit
by sunlight—stakes its claim,

chrysalis of history spooled tight
as a movie plot. Inside: maybe

a monarch. Maybe a tiger
moth.

The World is a Scented Handkerchief

after Shakir Li'aibi

The world is a moonlit rib,
      a disheveled vigil, a shackled

clock. The world is greedy
      geography, empty bells,

unripened tides, breathless
      shells on a desert beach.

The world is a newborn
      nun. The world is a fluttering

gun. The world is extinguished
      chants, listless ships, bleeding

thieves. It is clouded vowels,
      the taste of sound on the tongue

of a young girl. The world
      is every word unfurled.

The Week After

November 2016

I bite my tongue.
Not figuratively—

as in holding back
about the election—

but literally, while
eating a baguette

in Panera Bread.
The metallic taste.

The white napkin
tinged with bright

blood.

~

There is an earthquake,
then a tsunami warning.

An actual earthquake
in New Zealand where

my grown stepdaughter
lives. My husband and I

scour the internet for news.
Rebecca sends a video

from the hills where she
has evacuated at 2 a.m.

Below, the lights of
Christchurch are tiny,

hopeful eyes.

~

My friend is getting
a new roof. Workers

crack the skylight
as she steps out

of the shower. Bits
of debris drift down

onto her wet shoulders.
She looks up.

The sky is falling.

~

I think of my youngest
daughter's Muslim friend,

born in the U.S., who has
been told *Go back to where*

you came from. Her mother
marvels at my daughter's

love of Persian food.
She's used to keeping

frozen pizza on hand
for other kids. Last fall

she knocked on our door
and surprised us with

foil-covered dishes
of biryani chicken, curried

potatoes, basmati rice.
They were spicy and delicate

and warmed us on a cold night.

~

I think of my son's trans
classmate who works

at the grocery checkout.

~

I think of my brilliant
engineering student

whose hidden disability
makes it difficult for her

to spell her own name.

~

Two presidents ago
I had a student who

was living in his car.
His stepfather had

kicked him out of
the house. When

temperatures dipped,
he slept in the kitchen

of the Pizza Hut where
he washed dishes.

I made phone calls.
I wrote letters.

They weren't enough.
With 15 credits to go,

he withdrew from school.

~

I have pain in a molar
and am convinced

I need a root canal.
The dentist tells me

the phone has been
ringing nonstop.

It's the election,
she says. *Everyone*

is grinding their teeth
and clenching their jaws.

She files down a tooth
to adjust my bite.

The pain subsides.

~

I am driving my daughter
to a college interview.

She is a high school senior.
Her world is a blank map.

We stop at McDonald's
for coffee. I go to the restroom.

When I return, a man is yelling
comments about her body

and clothing. *Nice boots,
girl,* he says, looking her

up and down and grunting
Mm-hm. As we start to leave,

he stumbles out to the parking lot
and sits on the curb by our car.

I ask a male customer
to make sure we get out safely.

He agrees, seems proud to help,
as if he's been anointed.

We hurry past the man as he yells,
Hey girl, hey! Driving away,

I talk to my daughter about
being a woman, about feeling

vulnerable, about staying safe.
I talk to my daughter about

the privilege that allowed
me to enlist the protection

of a complete stranger.
It's not fair, she says.

It's not fair.

~

It has been one week.
A man comes to my office.

He looks familiar. I realize
he's the former student

who was living in his car.
His voice is deeper now.

He tells me he has been
working full-time. He tells me

he has re-enrolled to finish
his degree. We set up

his schedule for the spring.
He registers for sociology,

anthropology, Spanish,
two literature classes.

In his palm, I press the
the gift I give all my English

majors, a temporary tattoo.
He reads it out loud:

Metaphors Be with You.

Once you've seen a bird in your house,

you can never not see a bird in your house.
Every rustling paper, every curtain twisting

in a breeze, every shadow on a ceiling
is a frantic, fluttering bird. One winter we had

three in three weeks. I came home to find
our typically docile calico in the kitchen

feasting on a dead robin, her teeth bared,
face pasted with feathers. The house was sealed,

no obvious holes in the siding, windows,
or chimney, not like those buildings ripped open

by storms—giant dollhouses dripping
with insulation, beds and tables still in place,

paintings teetering over sofas. Don't get me
wrong—I'd never welcome destruction.

But I like to glimpse the cross-section
of others' lives. Through the rowhouse wall

we share with neighbors, we don't hear
voices, but sometimes there's a low rumbling

that would barely register a 1.0 on the conversation
Richter scale. Most mornings we hear their shower

pulsing behind our bed. Less than a foot away
a naked man is working his hair into a lather—

just once, I'm sure, because no one
believes those shampoo instructions telling us

to rinse and repeat, do they? When I was a child
we always rented one Days Inn motel room

for our family of four, and my parents hung a sheet
between their bed and ours, a makeshift partition.

I think this is true and not something I saw on TV.
Or maybe I just want to believe they liked each other

once. There are a million years between *is* and *was*,
are and *were*. It's no accident that houses have stories.

Ours has a foundation made of blocks. Sometimes
light squeezes through the cracks. Sometimes a bird.

Porpoises

Slick as oil, they stitch
        the waves, scalloped

edge of a black doily.
        On the horizon

of the heart monitor,
        my father's rhythm

lifts and dips.
        ICU. *I see you.*

But I haven't seen him
        in years. The doctors

will—what? *remove?*
        unplug? disconnect?

him from life support.
        What came first,

the brain bleed or the fall?
        How many days

was he unconscious
        on the floor? How many

decades was he disconnected
        from the world?

Father and daughter,
        the *r* a liquid consonant

absorbed by air, such a small
        role in each word.

As the oldest, I am executor.
        I am executioner.

Porpoise, like purpose:
        the *why*. I follow the blip

of fins in the distance
        until they grow faint,

then disappear. The sea
        flatlines beneath the sky.

After/Before

An artist friend has traded
  detailed scenes of farms

and streams for small fields
  of color during quarantine.

Rothko Postcards, he calls
  these gestures of sky and wheat.

My late mother-in-law
  once confessed to me

she'd had a near affair
  when my husband was young.

The man, also married,
  was superintendent of schools.

We were this close, she said,
  squeezing between her fingers

an invisible precious stone.
  She sat with him in the front seat

of her blue Buick in the board of ed
  parking lot to say she was choosing

her current life—
  then drove home to dress

the dinner salad with oil and vinegar
  the way I'd see her do decades later,

quick flicks of her wrists
  like brushstrokes in the kitchen air.

Square of green, square of blue.
        Square of orange, square of red.

Representational, abstract. Sunrise.
        Sunset. Hard dash of the horizon—

below/above, after/before—
        the independent clause of regret.

The Strip Mall of Second Chances

My daughter's pediatrician has been arrested
for writing Oxycodone prescriptions
for her 24-year-old lover. She's married
with two teenage kids, but that, of course,
isn't the issue—the issue is the drugs
and young man who sold them
to support his own habit, the young man
who no doubt told her everything
she needed to hear to erase two decades
of assembly line strep throat swabs
and ear infections, after-hours calls
about conjunctivitis and croup,
the rabbit warren of windowless,
florescent-lit exam rooms where,
after a ten-hour shift, she didn't know
if it had rained or snowed. A dull job,

really, but with such high stakes.
We all know at least one story
of a brain tumor misdiagnosed
as a migraine or a stomach bug
that was actually sepsis. A suspicious
pharmacist reported her, and now,
the papers say, she's lost her medical license.
There's a misdemeanor plea deal
in the works. No news on her marriage.
She's working as a cashier at a strip mall
department store, scanning items
and asking customers if they want to save
an extra 20% by opening a credit card.

I think back to those appointments.
She wasn't one for chitchat and barely
seemed to know my daughter's name.
I wonder if what I took for social awkwardness

was actually distraction, if she was
rushing to check a text from her lover.
Or maybe she was preoccupied
with the fear of getting caught.
I say the word *opioid* out loud
and try to think of other words
with three consecutive vowels.
Only *luau* and *paeon* come to mind.
Later: *pious*. How easy it is to judge

someone who blows up her life
in such spectacular fashion, a hat trick
of crime, family, and career. Most of us
ruin ourselves in smaller increments,
the way a fresh bar of soap slowly shrinks
to a sliver that slips down the drain.
We drink a little too much wine
at dinner or lash out at loved ones
with cruel precision as if we've spent
decades in school learning how to dole out—
and endure—micro-doses of pain.

Fury

When his name pops up in my inbox,
I nearly mistake it for spam: so generic,
he could be any man. But he was

the first boy I knew with his own car,
a 1973 baby blue Plymouth Fury
he polished and buffed till the chrome

winked like stars. I am tempted
to drag his message to the trash. This,
though, is social media—within a few

clicks, I see he's an accountant
with a sick child. There are fundraisers,
links to experimental drugs,

a photo of his seizure-prone son
slumped over the grocery cart seat
he has long outgrown. A wife waves

at the camera, her smile blurry.
Does she know he's contacting
old girlfriends at 2 a.m. from his

split level in LaGrange, Missouri?
Perhaps she prefers it to overheated rage.
The last Plymouth rolled off the line

more than a decade ago. But there will
always be the image in his profile.
There will always be the Fury.

Concealed

On the 75th day of quarantine, my true love
gives to me one handgun holster. Or at least

I think he does. The package, which arrives
with another containing a book, is meant

for a man on Edgar Street, a few blocks over
in this rural Pennsylvania borough.

The hollow black leather holster rests
on our ottoman with an item we did order:

a book by Slovenian philosopher Slavoj Žižek.
For the purpose of this poem, I want to change

the book to the one on my bedside table:
The Tradition by Jericho Brown. On the cover

are delicate flowers—inside, poems
about white hands on Black bodies.

Earlier this morning, I yelled at my husband.
I yelled at my husband about a coffee filter. Not

just any coffee filter, the large cylindrical filter
for the cold brew coffee pitcher I bought online

when stores began shutting down. You can't make
iced coffee by brewing a regular pot and pouring

it over ice. It will taste acidic and metallic,
like a lemony penny. But the filter, which is always

in the top drawer next to the refrigerator,
is gone. *Where did you put it?* I asked my husband.

Why do you think I moved it? he asks. *Who else*
would have moved it? I ask, my voice rising.

Maybe it slipped behind the drawer. No, it's too big.
Maybe it's in a cabinet. No, no, no, no. And then

he reaches up under the drawer, beyond the spatulas
and potato masher and there it is, a mesh cage

wedged behind the drawer's wooden lip. I am saying
drawer too many times, and the truth is,

I can't say the word at all. I grew up pronouncing it
the way my Rhode Island native mother said it:

draw. The dresser *draw,* the top *draw.* Like draw
a bath. Draw a gun. This week I completed an online

coronavirus contact tracer training. It certifies me
to follow up with patients and those they may have exposed.

What does corona mean? the instructor asked,
but we couldn't answer because it was recorded.

I may not know about RNA and R noughts,
but I know corona is a crown. We learn there are

four types of questions: closed and leading,
which are bad, and open and probing, which are good.

Have you been coughing? (closed)
You've been coughing, haven't you? (leading)

What symptoms have you been experiencing? (open)
How would you describe your cough? (probing)

The gun holster came with a card that says
Comfort starts here! and boasts of its concealment

features. The guy who ordered it is, I imagine,
one of the white men who refuses to wear a mask

because this is America, dammit.
Because Constitution. Because rights.

Are you privileged?
You're privileged, aren't you?

What does privilege mean to you?
How does your gun relate to privilege?

[How does your philosophy book relate to privilege?]
[How does your iced coffee maker relate to privilege?]

In the theatre they say if there's a pistol,
it must be fired in the last hour. I slip the package

in a blue mailbox in front of the post office,
mark it *misdelivered*. I have never held

a handgun, but I know that a bullet
in the body blossoms like a flower.

Anthimeria

using one part of speech as another

My sea gown scarf'd about me,
Hamlet said, verbing his attire.

My daughter likes her likes
on the socials and hearts pics

on the 'Gram. We front and friend,
rebrand brands, and rarely shop

local. Adults keep adulting,
sandwiched between parents

and kids. We don't read books—
we book flights or tourist trips

to the moon and Titanic's grave.
If submersible were only an adjective,

we wouldn't have lost five souls
in an underwater mini-van.

Man is used to being trapped in
cars, buildings, mines, caves.

Are we there yet? Are we? Are we?
You keep samin' when you oughta be

changin' goes the Nancy Sinatra song.
Every part of speech is a noun.

I want to person/place/thing you
from the cold, the blue, the gone.

Azul

Dupont Circle

Before we huddle under a café heater
in early spring sun and sample several

of the seventy tequilas, before we take a selfie
to send our grown kids in other cities

(No, higher so you can't see our double chins!),
before we walk thirty-two blocks—

a block for every year we've been together—
stopping just once to beg for the bathroom code

at Starbucks, before we notice the first nodule
of a cherry blossom peeking out

like a tiny pink tongue, before we make love
and doze on the starched hotel sheets,

before all of this, we're at the Phillips
for the Picasso show, his *Período Azul,*

where, next to "Two Women at a Bar,"
hangs a black and white photograph of his studio

from 1902 in which an early incarnation
of the painting rests upside-down on an easel

beside a pinned image of Rodin's "The Thinker,"
the musculature of the sculpture rhyming

with the women's sinewy shoulders and spines,
not unlike a poet pairing *musculature* and *sculpture,*

not unlike the elderly couple shuffling behind us
in the gallery, hunching before each blue scene,

their navy blazer and sweater bleeding
into a single garment, the *tick tick tick*

of her cane on the floor, the insistent whisper
of his portable oxygen machine.

About the Author

Erin Murphy is the author or editor of thirteen previous books, most recently *Taxonomies; Assisted Living*, a collection of demi-sonnets about caregiving; and *Fields of Ache*, a chapbook of centos. Her co-edited anthologies include *Bodies of Truth: Personal Narratives on Illness, Disability, and Medicine* and *Creating Nonfiction: Twenty Essays and Interviews with the Writers*, both of which won Foreword INDIES Book of the Year Awards. Her poems and essays have been published in *Women's Studies Quarterly, Rattle, North American Review, The Best of Brevity, Waxwing, One Art*, and *The Georgia Review* and featured on *The Writer's Almanac*. Her work has also been included in anthologies from Random House, Bloomsbury, Michigan State University Press, Terrapin Books, and Bedford/St. Martin's Press, among others. Her awards include a Dorothy Sargent Rosenberg Poetry Prize, The Normal School Poetry Prize, the Paterson Prize for Literary Excellence, the Rattle Poetry Prize Readers' Choice Award, and a Best of the Net award. She serves as Poetry Editor of *The Summerset Review*, Poet Laureate of Blair County, Pennsylvania, and Professor of English at Penn State University, Altoona College, where she has received the university-wide Alumni Award for Excellence in Teaching and the inaugural Mellon Academic Leadership Fellowship. Website: www.erin-murphy.com